Amazon WorkDocs User Guide

A catalogue record for this book is available from the Hong Kong Public Libraries.

Published in Hong Kong by Samurai Media Limited.

Email: info@samuraimedia.org

ISBN 9789888408078

Contents

What Is Amazon WorkDocs?

Amazon WorkDocs is a fully managed, secure, enterprise storage and sharing service with strong administrative controls and feedback capabilities that improve user productivity. Your files are stored in the cloud, safely and securely. Amazon WorkDocs even includes a synchronization application that always keeps selected folders on your local computer in sync with your cloud folders. Your files are only visible to you, and your designated contributors and viewers. Other members of your organization do not have access to any of your files unless you specifically grant them access.

You can share your files with other members of your organization for collaboration or review. The Amazon WorkDocs client applications can be used to view many different types of files, depending on the Internet media type of the file. Amazon WorkDocs supports all common document and image formats, and support for additional media types is constantly being added.

For more information, see Amazon WorkDocs.

Accessing

You use the client applications to access your files. Amazon WorkDocs offers several different client applications and utilities:

- A web application used for document management and review.
- Apps for mobile devices that support document review.
- A synchronization client that allows you to synchronize a folder on your Mac or Windows desktop with your Amazon WorkDocs files.

How to Get Started

To get a hands-on introduction to Amazon WorkDocs, complete the tutorial at Getting Started with Amazon WorkDocs.

Supported File Types

With Amazon WorkDocs, you can share the following file types for viewing and feedback:
- Microsoft Office Word
- Microsoft Office Excel
- Microsoft Office PowerPoint
- Text file with .txt extension
- PDF
- Office Open XML files
- .rtf, .xml, .xhtml+xml, and .xslt-xml
- OpenDocument Text files with extension .vnd.oasis.opendocument.text
- .javascript, .x-javascript, .x-sh, .x-python, .vnd.lotus-screencam, and .smil
- Text files with extension .html, .plain, .csv, .x-c, .x-c++, .x-makefile, .x-java-source, .x-java, .javascript, .x-perl-script, .x-python-script, .x-ruby-script, .php, .rtf, and .xml
- CAD files with extension .dwg, .vnd.dwg, and .autocad_dwg
- Image files with extension .jpeg, .png, .tiff, and .bmp

With the Amazon WorkDocs iOS clients, you can play audio and video files. Supported file types include .mp4, .3gp, .mov, .m4a, and .m4v. For more information about iOS clients, see Amazon WorkDocs iPad Client and Amazon WorkDocs iPhone Client.

Pricing

With Amazon WorkDocs, there are no upfront fees or commitments. You pay only for active user accounts, and the storage you use. For more information, go to Pricing.

Resources

The following related resources can help you as you work with this service.

- ** Classes & Workshops** – Links to role-based and specialty courses as well as self-paced labs to help sharpen your AWS skills and gain practical experience.
- ** AWS Developer Tools** – Links to developer tools, SDKs, IDE toolkits, and command line tools for developing and managing AWS applications.
- ** AWS Whitepapers** – Links to a comprehensive list of technical AWS whitepapers, covering topics such as architecture, security, and economics and authored by AWS Solutions Architects or other technical experts.
- ** AWS Support Center** – The hub for creating and managing your AWS Support cases. Also includes links to other helpful resources, such as forums, technical FAQs, service health status, and AWS Trusted Advisor.
- ** AWS Support** – The primary web page for information about AWS Support, a one-on-one, fast-response support channel to help you build and run applications in the cloud.
- ** Contact Us** – A central contact point for inquiries concerning AWS billing, account, events, abuse, and other issues.
- ** AWS Site Terms** – Detailed information about our copyright and trademark; your account, license, and site access; and other topics.

Getting Started with Amazon WorkDocs

Amazon WorkDocs is based on organizations and include the users who belong to the organization, as well as information about each user's folders and documents. Before you can start using Amazon WorkDocs, you must complete the following tasks.

Topics

- Step 1: Get Invited
- Step 2: Register
- Step 3: Start Using Amazon WorkDocs

Step 1: Get Invited

Participation in an Amazon WorkDocs organization is by invitation only. Your Amazon WorkDocs administrator creates an organization and invites the users to join that organization. An administrator can also enable other people in the organization to invite others to join the organization.

You will receive communication from your Amazon WorkDocs administrator with information about how to register (if necessary) and where to download the client applications from.

Step 2: Register

When you receive your invitation to join an Amazon WorkDocs organization, you may need to complete your user registration. Completing your registration involves setting your user information, which includes the following:

- First name
- Last name
- Password

You can change your profile photo, timezone, and password from your **Profile** page after you complete your registration. For more information, see My Account.

Step 3: Start Using Amazon WorkDocs

After the previous steps are complete, you can begin working with Amazon WorkDocs using one of the client applications. There are several clients used for document collaboration. Additionally, there is a document synchronization client that enables you to synchronize a folder on your Mac or Windows desktop with your Amazon WorkDocs files. For more information, see Amazon WorkDocs Clients.

Amazon WorkDocs Clients

Amazon WorkDocs provides client applications for document collaboration. With an Amazon WorkDocs client, users can view and provide feedback about shared files. Choose from a web client or clients for Android and iOS.

Additional clients provide the following options:

- Open and edit a file from the web application with one click using the Amazon WorkDocs Companion app. For more information, see Adding and Editing Files.
- Synchronize your desktop folder to Amazon WorkDocs using the Sync Client. For more information, see Amazon WorkDocs Sync Client.
- Microsoft Windows users can access their Amazon WorkDocs content in Windows File Explorer using Amazon WorkDocs Drive. For more information, see Amazon WorkDocs Drive.

Topics

- Amazon WorkDocs Web Client
- Amazon WorkDocs Android Tablet Client
- Amazon WorkDocs Android Phone Client
- Amazon WorkDocs iPad Client
- Amazon WorkDocs iPhone Client
- Amazon WorkDocs Sync Client
- Amazon WorkDocs Drive
- Amazon WorkDocs Client Overview

Amazon WorkDocs Client Overview

You can use the following features with the Amazon WorkDocs clients. **People**
The **People** tab displays the owner of a file and the people that the file is shared with. People are identified by role: owner, viewer, or contributor.

From the web client, you can share a file, share a folder, or send a message. **Feedback**
The **Feedback** displays the feedback that was saved for a file. The overall feedback appears at the top, and the context-specific feedback appears in order from the beginning to the end of the file. You can scroll through the feedback and select a specific piece of feedback to review. When you select a piece of feedback, the portion of the file that the feedback belongs to is scrolled into view. Similarly, if you scroll through the file and select a highlighted portion of the file, the feedback for that portion is scrolled into view and selected.

The procedure for giving feedback on a file varies slightly depending on which collaboration client you are using. For more information about giving feedback with a specific client, see the documentation for the client. **Activity**
The **Activity** tab displays the history of activity for a file, such as uploads, when feedback was requested, and when feedback was saved. You can view the version of a file that was uploaded.

Amazon WorkDocs Web Client

The Amazon WorkDocs web client is a fully functioning website that allows you to upload, download, and organize your online Amazon WorkDocs document store. It is also used to view and comment on your documents and documents from others. The web client can display previews for many different types of files, depending on the internet media type of the document.

Topics

- System Requirements
- Log In
- Web Client View
- Folders
- Adding and Editing Files
- Hancom Online Editing
- Open with Office Online
- Locking and Unlocking Files
- File Versions
- Renaming Files
- Moving Files
- Deleting Files
- Downloading Files
- Sharing a Folder or File
- Sending a Message
- Share a Link
- Giving Feedback
- Viewing the Activity Feed
- Viewing File Properties

System Requirements

The Amazon WorkDocs web client requires one of the following web browsers:

- Google Chrome version 30 or later
- Mozilla Firefox ESR version 24.6 or later
- Mozilla Firefox version 30 or later
- Apple Safari version 7 or later
- Microsoft Internet Explorer 10 or later

Log In

When you launch the Amazon WorkDocs web client, log in with your organization name, user name, and password. The organization name and user name are provided in the welcome email that you received from your Amazon WorkDocs administrator. Your password was established when you completed the initial user registration. For more information, see Step 2: Register.

If your Amazon WorkDocs administrator has enabled multi-factor authentication (MFA) for your organization, you are also prompted for a passcode to complete your login. Your Amazon WorkDocs administrator provides information about how to obtain your passcode.

Enabling Single Sign-On

Amazon WorkDocs allows you to access Amazon WorkDocs from a computer that is joined to the same directory that Amazon WorkDocs is registered with, without having to enter your credentials separately. If your Amazon

WorkDocs administrator has enabled single sign-on for your organization, you might need to take additional steps to enable your web browser to support single sign-on. For more information, see Single Sign-On for Internet Explorer and Google Chrome and Single Sign-On for Firefox in the *AWS Directory Service Administration Guide*.

Note
Single sign-on only works when used on a computer that is joined to the AWS Directory Service directory. It can't be used on computers not joined to the directory.

Web Client View

The Amazon WorkDocs web client provides the following basic views.

Topics

- Navigation View
- File View

Navigation View

The following is the layout of the Amazon WorkDocs web client navigation view.

http://docs.aws.amazon.com/workdocs/latest/userguide/images/web_nav_view.PNG

1 - Files Pane

2 - Folder Navigation Controls

3 - Content Controls

4 - Action Controls

5 - View Pane

6 - User Control Pane

Files Pane

The files pane contains the following controls.

Topics

- My Docs
- Collaborate
- Activity Feed
- Search

My Docs

Displays your root folder. This folder contains the following sections:

- **My Docs**
- **Favorites**
- **Recycle bin**

Collaborate

Displays a list of the files that need collaboration, including files that are shared, awaiting feedback, or out for review. This folder contains the following sections:

- **Shared with me**
- **Awaiting my feedback**
- **Out for review**

Activity Feed

Displays a list of state changes for files and folders.

Search

Enables you to search for files and folders.

Folder Navigation Controls

My Docs

Displays all the files in your **My Documents** folder.

Favorites

Displays the files that you marked as favorites.

Recycle Bin

Displays the folders and files that have been deleted. Deleted folders and files are moved to the Recycle Bin and are kept there for a minimum of 30 days so they can be recovered as needed.

To restore a file or folder that is in your Recycle Bin, select the file or folder, then choose the **Restore** icon from the header.

To permanently delete an item that is in your Recycle Bin, select the file and folder, then choose the **Recycle Bin** icon.

You can empty your Recycle Bin by de-selecting all items and choosing the **Recycle Bin** icon and **Empty Recycle Bin**.

Shared with me

Displays a list of the files that have been shared with you.

Awaiting my feedback

Displays a list of the files for which your feedback has been requested.

Out for review

Displays a list of the files that you have shared with others.

Content Controls

The content controls provide controls for creating folders and uploading files and folders.

You can also drag and drop files into the web client.

Action Controls

The action controls allow users to take specific actions on files and folders, including lock, edit, share, favorite, and menu.

Lock
Allows you to lock the file to prevent it from being edited by other users. If the file is locked by you, only you can change the file. This feature is not available for folders. For more information, see Locking and Unlocking Files.

Edit
Allows you to edit a file with one click. When you choose **Edit**, the file opens in the native app and you can immediately start editing the file. The changes made to the file are saved automatically to Amazon WorkDocs. This feature is not available for folders. For more information, see Adding and Editing Files.
When you choose **Edit** for the first time and the Companion App for editing isn't installed yet, you see a message and a link to install the app. Once installed, the application works automatically the next time you choose **Edit**.

Share by invite
Allows you to share a folder or file with other users by inviting them. For more information, see Folders.

Share a link
Allows you to share a folder or file with other users by sharing a link with them. For more information, see Share a Link.

Favorite
Allows you to mark a file or a folder as a favorite.

Folder Menu

To display the folder menu, choose the three-dot icon on the folder line. The folder menu is displayed as a dropdown.

The folder menu gives you access to the following folder commands:

Open
Allows you to open a folder and see files in it.

Show activity
Allows you to see all activities related to the folder. For more information, see Viewing the Activity Feed.

Delete
Allows you to delete the folder. For more information, see Deleting a Folder.

Rename
Allows you to rename the folder. For more information, see Renaming a Folder.

Move
Allows you to move the folder. For more information, see Moving a Folder.

File Menu

To display the file menu, choose the three-dot icon on the file line. The file menu is displayed as a dropdown.

The file menu gives you access to the following folder commands.

Open
Allows you to open a folder and see files in it.

Show activity
Allows you to see all activities related to the folder. You can narrow your search by selecting filter options. For more information, see Viewing the Activity Feed.

Download

Allows you to download the file. For more information, see Downloading Files.

Delete

Allows you to delete the file. For more information, see Deleting Files.

Rename

Allows you to rename the file. For more information, see Renaming Files.

Move

Allows you to move the file. For more information, see Moving Files.

More

Contains the following sections:

- **Allow/Disallow Downloads**: Allows or prevents users from downloading a file.
- **Disable Feedback**: Prevents users from leaving feedback or comments on a file.

View Pane

The view pane displays the files and folders.

To get to an existing folder, click the folder name and the contents of the folder are displayed. You can see your current folder location in the breadcrumb trail at the top of the view pane. You can get to any folder in the hierarchy by selecting the folder name in the breadcrumb trail.

To open a file, click the file name and the file opens in the file view.

User Control Pane

The user control pane provides the following controls.

Topics

- Favorites
- About Us
- Support
- My Account
- Administration
- Logout

Favorites

This section, marked by a star icon, contains all the files and folders that have been marked as favorites.

About Us

This section, marked by the **i** icon, contains the blog and download app controls.

- **Blog ** opens the Amazon WorkDocs blog.
- **Download Apps** opens the Amazon WorkDocs client app download page.

Support

This section, marked by the **?** icon, contains feedback, forums, and help controls.

- **Feedback** allows users to give feedback.
- **Forums** opens the AWS discussion forums.
- **Help** opens the help documentation for Amazon WorkDocs.

My Account

You can update your user profile in the **My Account** section of the Amazon WorkDocs web client by clicking on your name in the Amazon WorkDocs user control pane. A sliding right panel appears where you can change the following items:

- Your profile photograph.
- Timezone.
- Password. This applies to cloud directories only. To change your password in a connected directory, contact your system administrator.

You cannot use the web client to change your name or email address. To change these, contact your Amazon WorkDocs administrator.

Administration

Note
This control is only available to Amazon WorkDocs administrators.

This control displays the administration dashboard. For more information, see Administration Dashboard in the *Amazon WorkDocs Administration Guide*.

Logout

This control logs you out of the Amazon WorkDocs web client.

File View

The following is the layout of the Amazon WorkDocs web client file view.

```
http://docs.aws.amazon.com/workdocs/latest/userguide/images/web_file_view.PNG
```

1 - File Navigation Controls

2 - Content and Action Controls

3 - File View Pane

4 - File Control Pane

File Navigation Controls

Use the file navigation controls to move back to the navigation view. To get to back to the navigation view, choose the root folder in the navigation controls area.

Content and Action Controls

Use the content and action controls to search within a file, lock a file, edit a file, share by link or invite, mark a file as a favorite, and download a file.

The menu section contains the following options:

- **Show activity** - Allows you to see the activity related to the files.
- **Upload new version** - Allows you to upload a new version of the file.
- **Delete** - Allows you to delete a file.
- **Disallow downloads** - Prevents you from downloading a file.
- **Disable feedback** - Prevents you from commenting on a file.

File View Pane

The file view pane contains the file display.

File Control Pane

Use the file control pane to view the people that the file has been shared with, give feedback on the file, view the past activity on the file, and view and update the file properties.

You can filter the comments on the file based on file versions and users who have commented on the files. You can also select to show draft comments, published comments, resolved comments, unresolved comments, and comments that mention your name.

For more information, see the following topics:

- People
- Feedback
- Activity

- Viewing File Properties

People

The **People** tab displays the owner of a file and the people that the file is shared with. People are identified by role: owner, viewer, or contributor. From the web client, you can share a file, share a folder, or send a message. This section also lets you change the permission of the user.

Feedback

Feedback displays the feedback that was saved for a file. The overall feedback appears at the top, and the context-specific feedback appears in order from the beginning to the end of the file. You can scroll through the feedback and select a specific piece of feedback to review. When you select a piece of feedback, the portion of the file that the feedback belongs to is scrolled into view. Similarly, if you scroll through the file and select a highlighted portion of the file, the feedback for that portion is scrolled into view and selected. The procedure for giving feedback on a file varies slightly depending on which collaboration client you are using. For more information about giving feedback with a specific client, see Amazon WorkDocs Clients.

Filter

Allows you to filter the comments on the file based on file versions and users who have commented on the files. You can also select to show draft comments, published comments, resolved comments, unresolved comments, and comments that mention your name.

Folders

The following topics discuss how you can manipulate and manage folders in the Amazon WorkDocs web client.

Topics

- Creating a Folder
- Renaming a Folder
- Moving a Folder
- Deleting a Folder
- Sharing a Folder

Creating a Folder

To create a folder

1. In the web client, open the folder in which to create the new folder.

2. Choose the **Create Folder** icon, enter the name of the folder, and choose **Create It**.

Renaming a Folder

You can change the name of a folder by performing the following steps.

To rename a folder

1. In the web client, open the folder that contains the folder to be renamed.

2. Choose the three-dot icon in the folder line to display the folder menu.

3. In the folder menu, choose **Rename**.

4. Enter the new name and press the Enter key.

Moving a Folder

When you move a folder, all of the files and folders within the folder are moved along with it.

To move a folder

1. In the web client, open the folder that contains the folder to be moved.

2. Choose the three-dot icon in the folder line to display the folder menu.

3. In the folder menu, choose **Move**.

4. In the **Move** dialog box, navigate to the target folder and choose **Move**.

Deleting a Folder

You can delete a folder in one of three ways. When you delete a folder, the folder is moved to the Recycle Bin. If there are files or other folders in the folder, they are moved to the recycle bin as well.

To delete a folder

- In the web client, open the folder to be delete, choose the three-dot icon to open the folder menu, and choose **Delete**.

Sharing a Folder

You can share a folder with other users in your organization. When you share a folder, all files and subfolders within that folder are available to the users with whom the folder is shared. If new files or subfolders are added to the folder, the shared users also have access to the new files.

To share a folder with other users

1. In the web client, open the folder that contains the folder to be shared.

    1. In the document control pane, choose **People**, **Share**.

    2. To display the folder menu, choose the three-dot icon. In the folder menu, choose **Share**.

2. In the **Share** dialog box, start typing the first or last name of the person in your organization that you want to share the folder with, and select the desired name when it is displayed in the list. If your Amazon WorkDocs administrator has authorized you to share folders with people outside your organization, you can also enter email addresses for external people and add them to the list of people with whom to share the folder.

    Repeat this step for any others with whom to share the folder.

3. Enter a personal message (if desired) of no more than 2048 characters, and choose if the folder is read-only. If the folder is not read-only, the users can upload new files or new versions of existing files to the folder.

4. Choose **OK**.

An email is sent to the people notifying them that a folder has been shared with them. The email includes a web link to the folder and the personal message that was entered, if one was specified. The users, along with their assigned role, are also added to the **People** tab. If you receive an error message indicating that you cannot share a folder with people outside of your organization, your administrator has not authorized you to invite new users to the organization. Contact your Amazon WorkDocs administrator for assistance.

Adding and Editing Files

To add a file to your documents, perform the following steps.

To add one or more files

1. In the web client, open the folder in which to place the file.

2. Choose the up-arrow upload icon, and select the file or files to be added.

You can also add files by dragging and dropping files from your computer into the web client. File drag-and-drop is not supported in all web browsers.

To upload a new version of a file

1. In the web client, open the file.

2. Click on the three-dot icon, then choose **Upload New Version** and select the new version of the file to upload.

To open and edit a file with one click, use the Amazon WorkDocs Companion app. After you install the app, you can open a file instantly in its default app and save your changes automatically to Amazon WorkDocs. You don't need to manually download, save, and re-upload the file.

To use the app, you must meet the following requirements:

- You must have owner, co-owner, or contributor permissions for the file.
- Your operating system must be Windows 7 or later, or macOS 10.1 or later.
- You must have one of the following internet browsers:
    - Chrome
    - Firefox with Flash Player 10 or later
    - Internet Explorer with Flash Player 10 or later
    - Safari with Flash Player 10 or later
- The file type must be one of the following:
    - Microsoft Office Word
    - Microsoft Office Excel
    - Microsoft Office PowerPoint
    - PDF
    - Text file with a .txt file extension

To instantly open and edit a file with one click

1. In the web client, open the file.

2. Choose the down arrow in the upper right corner and choose **Edit**.

3. If the Amazon WorkDocs Companion app isn't installed, follow the prompts to install it.

4. After installing the app, the file opens automatically in the default desktop app that is installed on your computer.

5. Edit the file in its app.

6. When you're done, choose **Save** to automatically save your changes to Amazon WorkDocs as a new file version.

Hancom Online Editing

Hancom Online Editing lets you create Microsoft Office files (`.docx`, `.pptx`, and `.xlsx`) from the Amazon WorkDocs web application. You can also co-author and collaboratively edit `.docx`, `.doc`, `.pptx`, `.ppt`, `.xlsx`, and `.xls` files.

When you edit a document with Hancom Online Editing, other users with edit permissions can join the live collaborative session to edit the document with you in real time. Files edited with Hancom Online Editing are saved automatically in Amazon WorkDocs.

To use Hancom Online Editing, your site administrator must enable the feature for your Amazon WorkDocs site. For more information, site administrators can see Enabling Hancom Online Editing.

Creating a New File

Use Hancom Online Editing to create new Microsoft Office files from the Amazon WorkDocs web application.

To create a new file with Hancom Online Editing

1. In the web application, under **MyDocs**, choose **New**.
2. Choose the file type: **Document**, **Spreadsheet**, or **Presentation**.
3. Edit the file in the web application.
4. When you are done editing, choose **Save & Exit**. The file is saved with a generic file name, such as **New Document**.
    1. Rename the file as needed. For more information, see Renaming Files.

Editing a File

Use Hancom Online Editing to edit Microsoft Office files and join live collaborative editing sessions from the Amazon WorkDocs web application.

To edit an Office file with Hancom Online Editing

1. In the web application, view the file. You can also open it in the file browser view.
2. Choose **Edit**.
3. Edit the file in the web application.

To join a live collaborative session

You can join another user in a live collaborative editing session to edit an Office file using Hancom Online Editing.

1. In the web application, view the file. You can also open it in the file browser view.
2. Choose **Live edit**.
3. Edit the file in the web application with the other users.

Open with Office Online

Open with Office Online lets you co-author and collaboratively edit Microsoft Office files (.docx, .pptx, and .xlsx) from the Amazon WorkDocs web application. When you edit a document with Office Online, other users with edit permissions can join the live collaborative session to edit the document with you in real time. Files edited with Office Online are saved automatically in Amazon WorkDocs.

Prerequisites

To use Open with Office Online, you need a Microsoft Office 365 **Work** or **School** account with a license to edit in Office Online, and your site administrator needs to enable the feature for your Amazon WorkDocs site. For more information, site administrators can see Enabling Open with Office Online.

For more information about getting a Microsoft Office 365 license, see Microsoft Office Licensing, Get the latest advanced features with Office 365, and Get the most from Office with Office 365.

Open with Office Online works with the Amazon WorkDocs web application in the most recent versions of Firefox, Chrome, Internet Explorer, and Safari.

Using Open with Office Online

After meeting the Prerequisites, you can use Open with Office Online to edit Microsoft Office files and join live collaborative editing sessions from the Amazon WorkDocs web application.

To edit a file with Office Online

Follow these steps to edit a Microsoft Office file using Open with Office Online.

1. In the web application, open the file or select it in the file browser view.

2. Choose **Edit**.

   - If this is your first time using Open with Office Online, or if it's been a while since you last used it, you are prompted to enter your Microsoft Office credentials.

3. The file opens in the web application for you to edit.

To join a live collaborative session

If another user is editing a Microsoft Office file using Open with Office Online, you can join them in a live collaborative editing session.

1. In the web application, open the file or select it in the file browser view.

2. Choose **Live edit**.

   - If this is your first time using Open with Office Online, or if it's been a while since you last used it, you are prompted to enter your Microsoft Office credentials.

3. The file opens in the web application for you to edit, along with other users.

Locking and Unlocking Files

You can lock a file to prevent others from overwriting your work while you're editing it. Collaborators can see a lock icon next to the file to know when it's locked. While it's locked, only the person who locked it can upload a new version.

Owners, co-owners, and contributors can lock files and send requests to unlock a file. Owners and co-owners can also unlock files, and contributors can unlock a file if they locked it.

To lock and unlock a file

1. Open the Amazon WorkDocs file to lock.

2. To lock the file, choose the down arrow in the upper-right corner and choose **Lock**.

3. To edit the file while it's locked, choose one of the following options:

   - Choose the down arrow in the upper-right corner, choose **Download**, and make your changes. When you're done making changes, open the file again in Amazon WorkDocs, choose the down arrow in the upper-right corner, and choose **Upload new version**.
   - Edit the file from the Amazon WorkDocs Sync Client.

4. To unlock the file, choose the down arrow in the upper-right corner and choose one of the following options:

   - If you made changes that you want to save, choose **Unlock and save changes**.
   - If you made changes that you don't want to save, choose **Unlock and discard changes**.
   - If you didn't make any changes, choose **Unlock**.

To send an unlock request

1. In the Amazon WorkDocs file, choose the down arrow in the upper-right corner and choose **Request unlock**.

2. In the **Request unlock** dialog box, enter a comment (optional) and choose **Send request**.

3. The request is sent to the person who locked the file, the file owner, and any co-owners.

File Versions

If more than one version of a file has been uploaded, you can select the version to view by performing the following steps:

To open a specific version of a file

1. In the web client, open the file.

2. Choose **Version** *X* **of** *X* and select the version of the file to view. If there is only one version of a file that has been uploaded, the **Version** *X* **of** *X* control is not displayed.

Renaming Files

You can change the name of a file by performing the following steps.

To rename a file

1. In the web client, open the folder that contains the file to be renamed.

2. To display the file menu, choose the three-dot icon on the file line.

3. In the file menu, choose **Rename**.

4. Type the new name and press the Enter key.

Moving Files

To move a file from one folder to another, perform the following steps.

To move a file

1. In the web client, open the folder that contains the file to be moved.

2. To display the file menu, choose the three-dot icon on the file line.

3. In the file menu, choose **Move**.

4. In the move dialog box, navigate to the folder you want to move the file to and choose **Move**.

Deleting Files

You can delete a file in one of two ways. Deleted files are moved to the Recycle Bin.

To delete a file

- Use one of the following ways:

  1. In the web client, open the file in the file view and choose **Delete** from the menu options.

  2. In the web client, open the folder that contains the file to be deleted in the navigation view, choose the menu options on the file line, and choose **Delete**.

Downloading Files

You can download a file in one of two ways.

To download a file

- Use one of the following ways:

    1. In the web client, open the file in the file menu and choose the down-arrow icon to download.

    2. In the web client, open the folder that contains the file to be downloaded and choose the three-dot menu icon to **Download**.

Sharing a Folder or File

You can share a folder or file with other users and groups both within and outside your organization. You can also revoke the share, and the users can remove themselves from the share.

Limits

- You can only share with directory groups, not email distribution lists.
- If your administrator configured Amazon WorkDocs with AD Connector, you can't share with users outside the directory.

Topics

- Share a Folder or File
- Revoke a Share
- Remove Yourself from a Share

Share a Folder or File

You can share a folder or file with other users and groups both within and outside your organization using **Share by invite**. In addition, you can specify the type of access permissions when inviting a user.

To share a folder or file with other users and groups

1. In the web client, open the folder or file.

2. In the control pane, choose **Share by invite**.

3. In the **Share by invite** dialog box, start typing the name of the person or group in your organization with whom to share, and select the desired name when it is displayed in the list. If your Amazon WorkDocs administrator has authorized you to share files with people outside your organization, you can also enter email addresses for external people and add them to the list of people with whom to share the folder or file.

   Repeat this step for any others you want to share the file with.

4. Select the desired permissions for the folder or file.
   Co-Owner
   The users/groups are co-owners of the file or files in the folder. They can rename and delete files, and share the file or files with others.
   Contributor
   The users/groups can provide feedback on the file or files in the folder.
   Viewer
   The users/groups can only view the file or files in the folder. They cannot provide feedback. External users have **Viewer** as the default permission, and this can't be changed unless they are converted from a **Guest** to regular **User** by an administrator.

5. Enter a personal message (if desired) of no more than 2048 characters, and select if feedback is requested. If feedback is requested, you can optionally specify a deadline for receiving feedback. **Note** Feedback can only be requested for files, not folders. Feedback can only be requested from users, not groups.

6. Choose **OK**.

An email is sent to the people notifying them that a file has been shared with them. The email includes a web link to the file, the personal message that was entered, and the feedback deadline, if one was specified. The users/groups, along with their assigned role, are also added to the People tab. If you receive an error message that indicates that you cannot share a document with people outside of your organization, your administrator has not authorized you to invite new users to the organization. Contact your Amazon WorkDocs administrator for assistance.

Revoke a Share

After you have shared a folder or file, you can remove a user or groups from the share.

To revoke a share

1. In the web client, open the folder or file.

2. In the control pane, choose **People**.

3. From the list of people that the folder or file is shared with, choose **Close** next to the user or group to remove from the share list.

4. In the confirmation dialog box, choose **Remove It**. The user or group is immediately removed from the share list.

Remove Yourself from a Share

After a folder or file has been shared with you, you can remove yourself from the share if desired.

To remove yourself from a share

1. In the web client, open the folder that contains the folder or file that has been shared with you.

2. Choose the arrow for the item and **Remove me from share**.

3. In the confirmation dialog box, choose **Yes, remove me**. You immediately lose access to the share.

Sending a Message

To send a message to the people with whom you have already shared a file, perform the following steps while viewing the document:

To send a message to others

1. In the web client, open the file.

2. In the right pane, choose the **People** icon and **Send a Message**.

3. Type your message and choose **OK**. Your message is sent to all of the people with whom the file is shared.
   Note
   By default, your email is sent from "Amazon WorkDocs <no-reply@amazon.awsapps.com>," an unmonitored email address. Contributor email addresses are not included.

Share a Link

You can copy hyperlinks to content stored in Amazon WorkDocs. Share file links with coworkers and external partners, both inside and outside your organization. Folder links can only be shared with internal site members.

You can configure file links to allow access to site members only, or to anyone on the internet. Site members can view, comment, update, and delete. Public links are restricted to viewing only. For additional security, you can set an expiration date and a 4-digit passcode for access to your content.

To share a link

1. In the web client, open the folder that contains the folder or file.

2. Choose the **Share a Link** icon.

3. In the **Share a Link** dialog box, copy the URL that is displayed by selecting it.

4. (Optional) Choose **Edit link settings** to set the following settings:
   Enable link
   Choose **On** or **Off**.
   Expiration date
   Type the date when the link expires. The link expires at midnight of the specified date.
   4-digit passcode
   Type a 4-digit numeric passcode that link recipients must enter for content access.
   Access
   Choose **Anyone can view** (file links only), **View only - internal**, or **View & comment - internal**.

5. Choose **Done**.

Giving Feedback

Other people in your organization can request feedback from you on specific files. You can add feedback to a file, or add a message about the entire file. You can also reply to feedback, give private feedback, and decline to give feedback.

You can see the files for which your feedback has been requested in your **Awaiting my Feedback** list. To request feedback, you can share your document with other people in your organization. For more information, see Sharing a Folder or File.

Topics

- Adding Feedback
- Declining Feedback
- Disabling Feedback
- Requesting the Ability to Add Feedback

Adding Feedback

You can add overall feedback that applies to the entire file, or add feedback on a specific portion of a file.

To add overall feedback

1. Open a document in Amazon WorkDocs.

2. In the right pane, choose **Feedback**, **Add Overall Feedback**.

3. Type your feedback and choose **Publish**. Your comment is uploaded to the server at the next opportunity.

To add feedback for a portion of a file

1. Open a document in Amazon WorkDocs.

2. Select the portion of the file on which to give feedback, and type your feedback in the right pane.

3. After you have entered your feedback, choose **Post**. This saves your feedback as a draft. You can edit or delete any of your feedback from the **Feedback** tab of the right pane.

To reply to feedback

Replies to comments are visually grouped together, sorted chronologically with the most recent comment on top, and include time stamps and user names. The number of replies are unlimited, and replies can be collapsed and expanded. If you download the file to your hard drive, all comments, including replies, are included.

1. In the right pane, choose **Feedback**.

2. Under the comment to which to reply, choose **Reply**.

3. Type your reply and choose **Post**.

To add private feedback

Private comments are only visible to the file owner and co-owners. They cannot be seen by contributors, unless you make a private reply to a contributor comment. If you download the file to your hard drive, they are not included. Replies to private comments are also marked private.

1. Underneath your comment, choose **Mark as Private**.

2. Choose **Post** and verify that your comment is marked **Private**.

To notify a user in feedback

You can notify a specific user in a comment to bring a user's attention to a specific comment. The user receives an email notification that includes the comment.

1. In the comment box, choose the @ button and then choose the user name from the list that appears. Or, type @ followed by the user name (for example, @username).

2. The user specified automatically receives an email that includes your comment and a link to view the file.

To format feedback

1. To bold a word, add ** before and after the word. (For example, **word**)

2. To italicize a word, add _ before and after the word. (For example, _word_)

3. To strikethrough a word, add ~before and after the word. (For example, ~word~)

To filter feedback

You can filter feedback to view specific comments that are the most important to you.

1. Open a document in Amazon WorkDocs.

2. In the right pane, choose the filter icon to the right of **Feedback**.

3. To view specific feedback, choose from any of the following filters:
   - **Version**
   - **User**
   - **Show**: Select the check box next to one or more of the following options:
     - **Draft comments**
     - **Published comments**
     - **Resolved comments**
     - **Unresolved comments**
     - **Comments that mention me**

4. Choose **Filter**.

To resolve feedback

You can hide comments from view by resolving them.

1. Open a document in Amazon WorkDocs.

2. In the right pane, choose **Feedback**.

3. Under each comment to hide, choose **Resolve**.

To show a resolved comment again, filter by **Resolved comments** and choose **Unresolve** under the comment.

To turn off email notifications

You can choose not to receive an email notification every time someone leaves a comment on a file.

1. Open a document in Amazon WorkDocs.

2. In the right pane, choose the gear icon in the upper-right corner.

3. Under **Notification Settings**, choose **Disable email notifications**.

Declining Feedback

You can decline to give feedback on any file for which you have received a feedback request. When you decline feedback, the file is removed from your **Awaiting my Feedback** list, and you can no longer view the file.

To decline feedback

1. In the web client, open the **Awaiting my Feedback** folder.

2. To display the feedback menu, click anywhere on the file line except the file name.

3. In the feedback menu, choose **Decline Feedback**.

You can also remove a file from the **Awaiting my Feedback** list without declining feedback.

To remove a file from your Awaiting my Feedback folder

1. In the web client, open the **Awaiting my Feedback** folder.

2. To display the feedback menu, click anywhere on the file line except the file name.

3. In the feedback menu, choose **Delete**.

Disabling Feedback

If you are the owner or co-owner of a file, you can lock the file to prevent it from receiving additional comments.

To disable feedback

1. In the right pane, choose **Feedback**.

2. Choose **Settings**, **Disable feedback for the document**.

Requesting the Ability to Add Feedback

If you have viewer access to a file and can't give feedback, you can request contributor access to add feedback.

To request ability to add feedback

1. Open the document.

2. Under the message **You don't have access to the feedback**, choose **Request Access**.

3. Type the justification for your request and choose **Request Access**.

The file owner receives an email notification about your request and grants you access. You receive an email that the file has been shared with you.

Viewing the Activity Feed

You can browse a log of recent activity around your Amazon WorkDocs content. Activities include views, comments, downloads, shares, locks, and deletions. You can see who changed a file and when it was changed. You can also search for a specific file, folder, or user name, and filter by activity type and date modified. If you are an administrator, you can view activities performed by all users of a site. For more information, see Site-wide Activity Feed.

To view the activity feed

1. In the web client, choose **Activity feed** and browse to view the latest activities.

2. To search and filter for specific activity, follow these steps:

    1. In the search box, type a file, folder, or user name.

    2. Choose **Filter**, then select **Activity Type** filters and choose a **Date Modified** option as needed.

    3. Choose **Apply**.

To see the activity feed of a file or folder, choose **Show Activity** from the file or folder menu.

Viewing File Properties

You can view the properties of a file by choosing the settings (gear) icon in the right pane of the file view. In this area, you can see the file type and size, created date and time, and the last modified date and time. To mute notifications, choose the **ON** button.

Amazon WorkDocs Android Tablet Client

The Amazon WorkDocs Android client application allows you to view, comment on, and download documents from your Amazon WorkDocs files. The Android app can also be used to view, give feedback on, and download other organization documents for which you have been given permissions.

Topics

- System Requirements
- Log In
- Android Tablet Client Navigation View
- Android Tablet File View
- Giving Feedback on a File
- Locking and Unlocking Files
- Viewing Offline Files

System Requirements

The Amazon WorkDocs Android tablet application requires one of the following:

- An Android tablet with Android 2.3.3 or later
- Kindle Fire HD 7 (2nd Gen)
- Kindle Fire HD 8.9 (2nd Gen)
- Kindle Fire HD 7 (3rd Gen)
- Kindle Fire HDX 7 (3rd Gen)
- Kindle Fire HDX 8.9 (3rd Gen)

Log In

The first time you launch the Amazon WorkDocs app, you need to log in with your organization name, user name, and password. The organization name and user name are provided in the welcome email you received from your Amazon WorkDocs administrator. Your password was established when you completed the initial user registration. For more information, see Step 2: Register.

If your Amazon WorkDocs administrator has enabled multi-factor authentication (MFA) for your organization, you are also prompted for a passcode to complete your login. Your Amazon WorkDocs administrator provides information about how to obtain your passcode.

Android Tablet Client Navigation View

The following is the layout of the Amazon WorkDocs Android tablet navigation view.

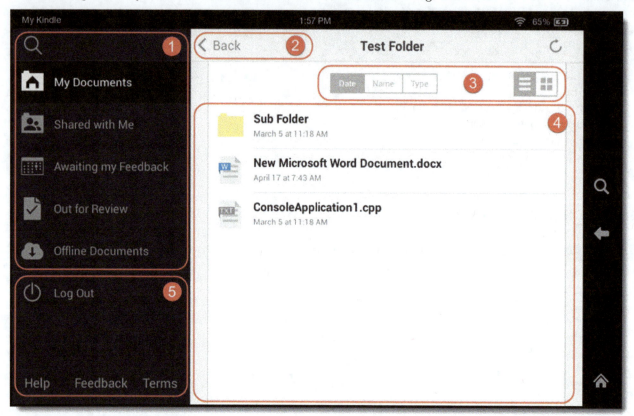

1 - Files Pane

2 - Navigation Controls

3 - View Controls

4 - View Pane

5 - User Control Pane

Files Pane

The files pane contains the following controls.

Topics

- Search
- My Documents
- Shared with Me
- Awaiting my Feedback
- Out for Review
- Recent Files
- Offline Documents

Search

Allows you to perform a text search of all of your documents, or the documents that have been shared with you.

My Documents

Displays your root folder.

Shared with Me

Displays a list of the files that have been shared with you.

Awaiting my Feedback

Displays a list of the files for which your feedback has been requested.

Out for Review

Displays a list of the files that you have shared with others.

Recent Files

Displays the files you have viewed most recently.

Offline Documents

Displays the files that have been downloaded to the device.

Navigation Controls

The folder navigation controls display the name of the parent of the current folder and can be used to navigate up in the folder hierarchy. You can move up one level in the folder hierarchy by choosing the name of the parent folder in the navigation controls area.

View Controls

You can view the items in the view pane in either tile view or list view. Change to list view by choosing the list view icon (≡) in the upper-right corner of the view pane. Change to tile view by choosing the tile view icon (⠿) in the upper-right corner of the view pane.

View Pane

The view pane displays the contents of the currently selected folder. To get to an existing folder, choose the folder, and the contents of the folder are displayed.

To view a document, choose the document and the document is displayed if it is of a type that the app can interpret and display. If the document cannot be displayed, a message saying so is displayed.

User Control Pane

The user control pane enables you to get access to help, give feedback on the client or service, and read the usage terms. Choose **Log Out** to log out of the Amazon WorkDocs client.

Android Tablet File View

The following is the layout of the Amazon WorkDocs Android tablet file view.

1 - File Navigation Controls

2 - Content Controls

3 - File View Pane

4 - File Control Pane

File Navigation Controls

You use the file navigation controls to move back to the navigation view. To get to back to the navigation view, choose **Back** in the navigation controls area.

Content Controls

You use the content controls to download a local copy of the file. For more information, see Viewing Offline Files.

File View Pane

The file view pane contains the file display.

File Control Pane

You use the file control pane to view the people that the file has been shared with, give feedback on the file, and view the past activity on the file. For more information, see the following topics:

- People
- Feedback
- Activity

Giving Feedback on a File

Other people in your organization can request feedback from you on specific files. You can add feedback to a file, or add a message about the entire file. You can also reply to feedback, give private feedback, and decline to give feedback.

You can see the files for which your feedback has been requested in your **Awaiting my Feedback** list.

Topics

- Adding Feedback
- Declining Feedback
- Disabling Feedback
- Requesting the Ability to Add Feedback

Adding Feedback

You can add overall feedback that applies to the entire file, or add feedback on a specific portion of a file.

To add overall feedback

1. Open a document in Amazon WorkDocs.

2. Open the ⊜ icon and choose **Leave a Quick Comment**.

3. Enter your feedback and choose **OK**. Your comment is uploaded to the server at the next opportunity.

To add feedback for a portion of a file

1. Open a document in Amazon WorkDocs.

2. To select the text on which to give feedback, choose an area of the text. You can then expand or contract the selection to include the desired text. When you have selected the text, choose **Comment**.

3. Enter your feedback and choose **OK**. This saves your feedback as a draft. You can edit or delete any of your drafts from the feedback view of the right pane. Feedback is saved and merged with the document on the server when you choose **Send** in the feedback view.

To reply to feedback

Replies to comments are visually grouped together, sorted chronologically with the most recent comment on top, and include timestamps and usernames. The number of replies are unlimited, and replies can be collapsed and expanded. If you download the file to your hard drive, all comments, including replies, are included.

1. In the right pane, choose **Feedback**.

2. Under the comment to which to reply, choose **Reply**.

3. Enter your reply and choose **Post**.

To add private feedback

Private comments are only visible to the file owner and co-owners. They cannot be seen by contributors, unless you make a private reply to a contributor comment. They are not included if you download the file to your hard drive. Replies to private comments are also marked private.

1. Underneath your comment, choose **Mark as Private**.

2. Choose **Post** and verify that your comment is marked **Private**.

To notify a user in feedback

You can notify a specific user in a comment to bring a user's attention to a specific comment. The user receives an email notification that includes the comment.

1. In the comment box, choose the @ button and then choose the username from the list that appears. Or, type @ followed by the username (for example, @username).

2. The user specified automatically receives an email that includes your comment and a link to view the file.

To format feedback

1. To bold a word, add ** before and after the word. (For example, **word**)

2. To italicize a word, add _ before and after the word. (For example, _word_)

3. To strike through a word, add ~before and after the word. (For example, ~word~)

Declining Feedback

You can decline to give feedback on any file for which you have received a feedback request. When you decline feedback, the file is removed from your **Awaiting my Feedback** list, and you can no longer view the file.

To decline feedback

1. Open the **Awaiting my Feedback** folder.

2. Click anywhere on the file line except the file name, to display the feedback menu.

3. In the feedback menu, choose **Decline Feedback**.

You can also remove a file from the **Awaiting my Feedback** list without declining feedback.

To remove a file from your Awaiting my Feedback folder

1. Open the **Awaiting my Feedback** folder.

2. Click anywhere on the file line except the file name, to display the feedback menu.

3. In the feedback menu, choose **Delete**.

Disabling Feedback

If you are the owner or co-owner of a file, you can lock the file to prevent it from receiving additional comments.

To disable feedback

1. In the right pane, choose **Feedback**.
2. Choose **Settings, Disable feedback for the document**.

Requesting the Ability to Add Feedback

If you have viewer access to a file and can't give feedback, you can request contributor access to add feedback.

To request ability to add feedback

1. Open the document.

2. Under the message **You don't have access to the feedback**, choose **Request Access**.

3. Enter the justification for your request and choose **Request Access**.

4. The file owner receives an email notification about your request and grants you access.

5. You receive an email that the file has been shared with you.

Viewing Offline Files

You can download any file that you are authorized to download by viewing the document and opening the download icon to download the current document to the device. If the document has already been downloaded, the download icon is highlighted .

You can view your offline files by choosing **Offline Documents** in the main menu. You can give feedback on a document even while offline. Your feedback is synchronized to the server the next time you have Internet access.

Amazon WorkDocs Android Phone Client

The Amazon WorkDocs Android phone client application allows you to view, comment on, and download documents from your Amazon WorkDocs files. The Android phone app can also be used to view, give feedback on, and download other organization documents for which you have been given permissions.

Topics

- System Requirements
- Log In
- Android Phone Main Menu
- Android Phone Folder View
- Android Phone File View
- Giving Feedback on a File
- Locking and Unlocking Files
- Viewing Offline Files

System Requirements

The Amazon WorkDocs Android phone client application requires the following:

- An Android phone with Android 4.0.3 or later

Log In

The first time you launch the Amazon WorkDocs app, you need to log in with your organization name, user name, and password. The organization name and user name are provided in the welcome email you received from your Amazon WorkDocs administrator. Your password was established when you completed the initial user registration. For more information, see Step 2: Register.

If your Amazon WorkDocs administrator has enabled multi-factor authentication (MFA) for your organization, you are also prompted for a passcode to complete your login. Your Amazon WorkDocs administrator provides information about how to obtain your passcode.

Android Phone Main Menu

The following is the layout of the Amazon WorkDocs Android phone main menu.

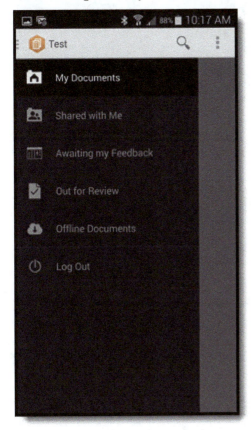

🔍 (Search)
Allows you to perform a text search of all of your documents, or the documents that have been shared with you.

My Documents
Displays your root folder.

Shared with Me
Displays a list of the files that have been shared with you.

Awaiting my Feedback
Displays a list of the files for which your feedback has been requested.

Out for Review
Displays a list of the files that you have shared with others.

Offline Documents
Displays the files that have been downloaded to the device.

Log Out
Log out of the app.

Android Phone Folder View

You can view folder items in either list view or grid view.

The following is the layout of the Amazon WorkDocs Android phone folder list view.

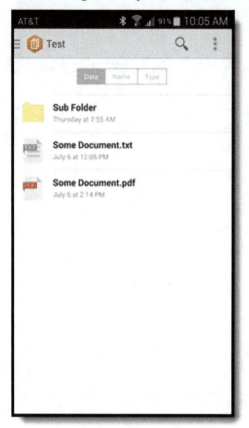

The following is the layout of the Amazon WorkDocs Android phone folder grid view.

While in grid view, change to list view by choosing the menu control (⋮) and **View as Grid**.

While in list view, change to grid view by choosing the menu control (⋮) and **View as List**.

Android Phone File View

The following is the layout of the Amazon WorkDocs Android phone file view.

Choose the download icon ⬇ to download the current document to the device. For more information, see Viewing Offline Files.

Choose the tab control (▭) to display the following controls. You use these controls to display different control views for the file.

⛊ - Displays the people view. For more information, see People.

💬 - Displays the feedback view. For more information, see Feedback.

🕔 - Displays the activity view. For more information, see Activity.

Amazon WorkDocs iPad Client

The Amazon WorkDocs iPad application allows you to view, comment on, and download documents from your Amazon WorkDocs files. The iPad app can also be used to view, give feedback on, and download other organization documents for which you have been given permissions.

Topics

- System Requirements
- Log In
- iPad Navigation View
- iPad File View
- Giving Feedback on a File
- Locking and Unlocking Files
- Viewing Offline Files
- Opening a File in Another iOS App to View or Edit
- Saving a File from Another iOS App to Amazon WorkDocs

System Requirements

The Amazon WorkDocs iPad application requires the following:

- iPad or iPad 2 with iOS 6.1.2 or later

Log In

The first time you launch the Amazon WorkDocs app, you need to log in with your organization name, user name, and password. The organization name and user name are provided in the welcome email you received from your Amazon WorkDocs administrator. Your password was established when you completed the initial user registration. For more information, see Step 2: Register.

If your Amazon WorkDocs administrator has enabled multi-factor authentication (MFA) for your organization, you are also prompted for a passcode to complete your login. Your Amazon WorkDocs administrator provides information about how to obtain your passcode.

iPad Navigation View

The following is the layout of the Amazon WorkDocs iPad navigation view.

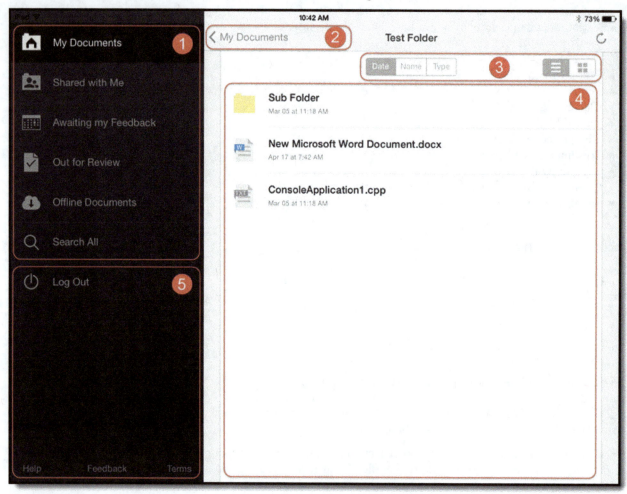

1 - Files Pane

2 - Navigation Controls

3 - View Controls

4 - View Pane

5 - User Control Pane

Files Pane

The files pane contains the following controls.

Topics

- My Documents
- Shared with Me
- Awaiting my Feedback
- Out for Review
- Recent Files

- Offline Documents
- Search All

My Documents

Displays your root folder.

Shared with Me

Displays a list of the files that have been shared with you.

Awaiting my Feedback

Displays a list of the files for which your feedback has been requested.

Out for Review

Displays a list of the files that you have shared with others.

Recent Files

Displays the files you have viewed most recently.

Offline Documents

Displays the files that have been downloaded to the device.

Search All

Allows you to perform a text search of all of your documents, or the documents that have been shared with you.

Navigation Controls

The folder navigation controls display the name of the parent of the current folder and can be used to navigate up in the folder hierarchy. You can move up one level in the folder hierarchy by choosing the name of the parent folder in the navigation controls area.

View Controls

You can view the items in the view pane in either tile view or list view. You change to list view by choosing the list view icon (≡) in the upper-right corner of the view pane. You change to tile view by choosing the tile view icon (⁚⁚) in the upper-right corner of the view pane.

View Pane

The view pane displays the contents of the currently selected folder. To get to an existing folder, choose the folder and the contents of the folder are displayed.

To view a folder, choose the folder and the contents of the folder are displayed.

To view a document, choose the document and the document is displayed if it is of a type that the app can interpret and display. If the document cannot be displayed, a message saying so is displayed.

User Control Pane

The user control pane enables you to get access to help, give feedback on the client or service, and read the usage terms. Choose **Log Out** to log out of the Amazon WorkDocs client.

iPad File View

The following is the layout of the Amazon WorkDocs iPad file view.

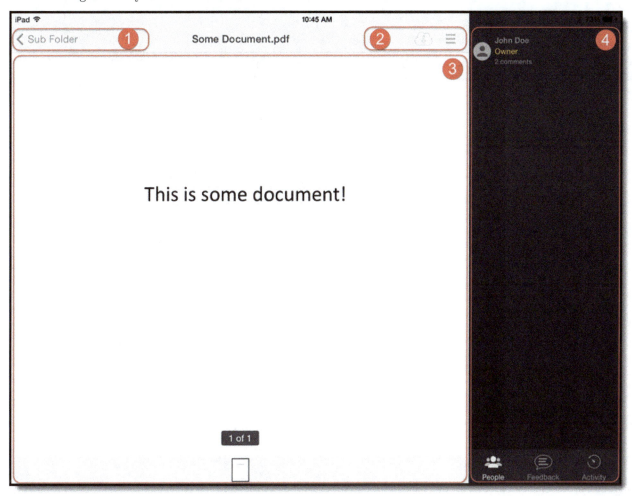

1 - File Navigation Controls

2 - Content Controls

3 - File View Pane

4 - File Control Pane

File Navigation Controls

You use the file navigation controls to move back to the navigation view. To get to back to the navigation view, tap the name of the parent folder in the navigation controls area.

Content Controls

You use the content controls to download a local copy of the file. For more information, see Offline Documents.

File View Pane

The file view pane contains the file display.

File Control Pane

You use the file control pane to view the people with whom the file has been shared, give feedback on the file, and view the past activity on the file. For more information, see the following topics:

- People
- Feedback
- Activity

Opening a File in Another iOS App to View or Edit

You can open an Amazon WorkDocs file in any other iOS app that supports file sharing. After opening the file, you can view or edit it in the other app, then save it back to Amazon WorkDocs.

To open a file in another iOS app

1. Open the Amazon WorkDocs file that you want to open in another app.

2. Choose **Menu**, **Share**, and then select the app to which to open the file.

3. If you want to save the file back to Amazon WorkDocs when you're done, see Saving a File from Another iOS App to Amazon WorkDocs.

Saving a File from Another iOS App to Amazon WorkDocs

You can save a file from any other iOS app that supports file sharing to Amazon WorkDocs. This makes the file available on other Amazon WorkDocs mobile apps, the web client, and the sync client.

To save a file from another iOS app to Amazon WorkDocs

1. Choose the file, photo, or attachment from any iOS app that supports file sharing.

2. Choose the export function in the app (this appears under different names depending on the app), and choose **WorkDocs iOS app**. **Note**
If **WorkDocs iOS app** doesn't appear in the list of apps, choose **Browse more** and slide the button to choose **WorkDocs iOS app**.

3. Select a target Amazon WorkDocs folder and choose **Save**.

Amazon WorkDocs iPhone Client

The Amazon WorkDocs iPhone client application allows you to view, comment on, and download your documents from your Amazon WorkDocs files. The iPhone app can also be used to view, give feedback on, and download other organization documents for which you have been given permissions.

Topics

- System Requirements
- Log In
- iPhone Main Menu
- iPhone Folder View
- iPhone File View
- Giving Feedback on a File
- Viewing Offline Files
- Opening a File in Another iOS App to View or Edit
- Locking and Unlocking Files
- Saving a File from Another iOS App to Amazon WorkDocs

System Requirements

The Amazon WorkDocs iPhone client application requires the following:

- An iPhone with iOS 7.0 or later

Log In

The first time you launch the Amazon WorkDocs app, you need to log in with your organization name, user name, and password. The organization name and user name are provided in the welcome email you received from your Amazon WorkDocs administrator. Your password was established when you completed the initial user registration. For more information, see Step 2: Register.

If your Amazon WorkDocs administrator has enabled multi-factor authentication (MFA) for your organization, you are also prompted for a passcode to complete your login. Your Amazon WorkDocs administrator provides information about how to obtain your passcode.

iPhone Main Menu

The following is the layout of the Amazon WorkDocs iPhone main menu.

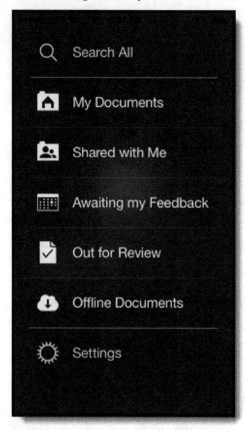

Search All
Allows you to perform a text search of all of your documents, or the documents that have been shared with you.

My Documents
Displays your root folder.

Shared with Me
Displays a list of the files that have been shared with you.

Awaiting my Feedback
Displays a list of the files for which your feedback has been requested.

Out for Review
Displays a list of the files that you have shared with others.

Offline Documents
Displays the files that have been downloaded to the device.

Settings
Change the app settings.

iPhone Folder View

You can view folder items in either list view or grid view.

The following is the layout of the Amazon WorkDocs iPhone folder list view.

The following is the layout of the Amazon WorkDocs iPhone folder grid view.

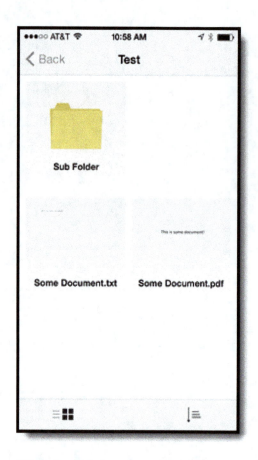

While in grid view, you change to list view by choosing the list view icon (▤) in the lower-left corner of the screen and **List**.

While in list view, you change to grid view by choosing the grid view icon (▥) in the lower-left corner of the screen and **Grid**.

iPhone File View

The following is the layout of the Amazon WorkDocs iPhone file view.

Open the download icon ⬇ to download the current document to the device. For more information, see Viewing Offline Files.

You use the controls at the bottom of the screen to display different control views for the file.

👥 - Displays the people view. For more information, see People.

💬 - Displays the feedback view. For more information, see Feedback.

🕐 - Displays the activity view. For more information, see Activity.

Amazon WorkDocs Sync Client

Amazon WorkDocs provides a client synchronization application that allows you to synchronize a folder on your desktop with the Amazon WorkDocs service. The local Amazon WorkDocs folder is a mirror of your Amazon WorkDocs My documents and Shared with me folders and subfolders in the cloud. If you add a file under your local Amazon WorkDocs folder, that file is automatically synchronized to your online Amazon WorkDocs My documents folder, in the background. Likewise, if you delete a file from your online Amazon WorkDocs My documents folder or one of its subfolders, the file is automatically removed from your local Amazon WorkDocs folder. This provides you with safe and secure off-site storage for your important files.

You can store any type of file in Amazon WorkDocs, except for those defined in Excluded Files and Folders. The Amazon WorkDocs collaboration clients can display previews for many different types of files, depending on the internet media type of the file. Support for additional media types is constantly being added.

Note
It can take up to a few minutes for syncing to begin, depending on your connection speed, bandwidth availability, and the size of the files you are syncing.

Topics

- System Requirements
- Installing the Sync Application
- Setting up the Sync Application
- Single Sign-On
- Changing the Amazon WorkDocs Account
- Excluded Files and Folders
- Sync Operation
- Using the Shared Sync Folder
- Deleting Shared Folders and Files
- Selecting a Sync Folder
- Uninstalling the Sync Application
- Troubleshooting Sync Issues

System Requirements

The Amazon WorkDocs sync application requires a computer running one of the following operating systems:

- Microsoft Windows 7, Windows 8, or Windows 10
- Microsoft Windows Server 2008
- Microsoft Windows Server 2012 R2 (with Microsoft AD, not Simple AD)
- macOS 10.10 or later

On all Windows clients, including all WorkSpaces, you must enable JavaScript in Internet Explorer. For more information, see How to enable JavaScript in a web browser?.

The sync application requires HTTPS access on port 443 for all IP addresses for AWS.

The sync application communicates with the Java engine. You can identify the port as follows:

- On Windows, locate the client.log file in the `%USERPROFILE%\AppData\Local\Amazon WorkDocs\ SyncClient` folder. Search for `http://127.0.0.1`. The port is specified as follows: `http://127.0.0.1: port`.
- On macOS, locate the sync-service.port file in the `/Users/user/Library/Application Support/Amazon WorkDocs/SyncClient` folder. The port is stored in plaintext.

The sync application supports local drives, but does not support non-local drives, including network drives and external USB drives.

Installing the Sync Application

The Amazon WorkDocs sync application is available for both Windows and macOS desktops.

To download and install the Amazon WorkDocs sync application using the console

1. Connect to the Amazon WorkDocs console

2. On the **Download apps** menu, choose **WorkDocs Companion**.

3. Under **Sync Files**, choose an option from the list of available installation options, and complete the installation.

To download and install the Amazon WorkDocs sync application for Windows

1. Download the Amazon WorkDocs sync application installer for Windows from https://d28gdqadgmua23. cloudfront.net/win/AmazonWorkDocsSetup.exe.

2. Run the installer. The Amazon WorkDocs sync application is downloaded, installed, and launched.

To download and install the Amazon WorkDocs sync application for macOS

1. Open the Amazon WorkDocs sync application for macOS from [https://d28gdqadgmua23.cloudfront.net/-mac/Amazon WorkDocs.pkg](https://d28gdqadgmua23.cloudfront.net/mac/Amazon WorkDocs.pkg).

2. Drag the Amazon WorkDocs Sync icon to the **Applications** folder.

3. Open the **Applications** folder and open **Amazon WorkDocs Sync**.

Setting up the Sync Application

The next step is registering the Amazon WorkDocs sync application. You can run the Amazon WorkDocs sync application on more than one local desktop. No matter how many desktops you synchronize, all of the files and folders in the sync folder are replicated on all of the desktops.

To complete the initial setup of the Amazon WorkDocs sync application

1. In the **Amazon WorkDocs Setup** dialog box, choose **Get Started**.

2. Type your Amazon WorkDocs site URL, which is provided by your Amazon WorkDocs administrator and choose **Next**.

3. Type your Amazon WorkDocs user credentials and choose **Sign In**.

4. The default for the sync folder is the `WorkDocs` folder in your user directory. This folder is created if it does not already exist. To choose a different folder, choose **Change** and select the folder. Choose **Next**. **Note** If you have previously installed the Amazon WorkDocs sync client, the initial folder may be renamed. We recommend using the default name to ensure that previous content is not overwritten.

5. Select the option to synchronize all files and folders or the option to synchronize only selected folders, and then choose **Next**.

6. Choose **Ok** to exit the setup program.

Note
The Amazon WorkDocs sync client is updated automatically when new versions are available.

Single Sign-On

The Amazon WorkDocs sync application does not require additional steps to enable single sign-on. If you experience any issues, restart the sync application to have the settings applied on your behalf.

Changing the Amazon WorkDocs Account

To change the Amazon WorkDocs account you have registered within the sync client, do the following:

Changing the Amazon WorkDocs account used in the sync client

1. Open the context (right-click) menu for the Amazon WorkDocs icon in your taskbar (or menu bar if you have a macOS).

2. Choose the gear icon to open **Preferences** and choose **Deregister this account**. Confirm your selection.

3. To register a new site, choose **Get Started** and go through the site registration steps.

Excluded Files and Folders

Any files or folders that meet the following criteria are not synchronized:

- Any file or folder name that starts with a period (.), such as the following:
  - ".lock"
  - ".~doctor.ppt"
  - "."
  - ".."
- Any file or folder name that starts or ends with a tilde (~), such as the following:
  - "hello.txt~"
  - "~WRD0000.tmp"
  - ".~doctor.ppt"
  - "~$filename.txt"
- Any file or folder name ending with ".tmp", such as the following:
  - "pptC407.tmp"
  - "~WRD0000.tmp"
- Any file or folder with one of the following names (the name and case must be an exact match):
  - Microsoft User Data
  - Outlook Files
  - Thumbs.db
  - Thumbnails
  - thumbnails
- Any file or folder name that includes any of the following characters:
  - * (asterisk)
  - / (forward slash)
  - \ (back slash)
  - : (colon)
  - < (less than)
  - (greater than)
  - ? (question mark)
  - | (vertical bar/pipe)
  - " (double quotes)
  - character code 202E (\202E)
- Any file/folder that has a trailing space (' ') or period ('.') character:
  - "filename "
  - "filename."
- Any file or folder name that is longer than 255 characters
- Any file that is greater than 5 TB

Sync Operation

After the Amazon WorkDocs sync application is installed and running, any non-excluded files in your local sync folder that you add, remove, or modify are automatically synchronized with your Amazon WorkDocs `My documents` folder.

Note
Moving files you own out of the sync folder deletes them from your Amazon WorkDocs file repository in the web client, mobile apps, and other devices where the Amazon WorkDocs sync client is installed.

File uploads and downloads that are in progress when you close the sync application are automatically resumed the next time you log in.

You can add, remove, or modify files while offline and these changes will be updated to your Amazon WorkDocs repository when the sync client connects the next time.

To see the upload and sync status of your files, choose the Amazon WorkDocs icon in the status notification tray on your computer. You also see a list of recently synced files as well as when it was synced.

Using the Shared Sync Folder

In addition to the files and folders that you own, the Amazon WorkDocs sync application also allows you to sync the files and folders that have been shared with you.

To sync files and folders that have been shared with you

1. Open the preferences dialog box for the Amazon WorkDocs sync application.

2. Choose **Enable Shared Folder Sync**, and then close the preferences dialog box.

A folder called **Shared With Me** is created in your Amazon WorkDocs sync folder that contains copies of all of the files and folders that have been shared with you.

Deleting Shared Folders and Files

To free up local storage space, you can delete a file or folder that has been shared with you in the **Shared with me** folder. There are two ways to do this, depending on where you want the file or folder deleted from.

To delete a file or folder from your desktop, but still allow it to be accessed in the **Shared with me** folder by other users, other devices, and the web client, delete it only from your computer. You can access it again from the **Shared with me** folder by re-selecting it from the **WorkDocs Selective Sync Settings** on your desktop.

If you permanently delete a file or folder in the **Shared with me folder** for all users, all of your devices, and the web client, it cannot be accessed again. You must have collaborator or co-owner permissions to do this.

To delete a file or folder from your computer only

- Delete it from the **Shared with me** folder on your desktop, or de-select it from the **WorkDocs Selective Sync Settings** on your desktop.

To delete a file or folder for all users and devices

1. Open the web client.

2. On the **Shared with me** tab, choose the file or folder to delete.

3. Choose **Delete**.

4. The file or folder appears in the **Recycle Bin** of your web client.

   - To restore the item, open the context (right-click) menu of the **Recycle Bin**, choose **Open**, right-click on the item, and choose **Restore**.

- To delete the item permanently, open the context (right-click) menu of the **Recycle Bin** and choose **Empty Recycle Bin**. **Note**
If you delete a file or folder from `My documents`, it is moved to the recycle bin on the web client. It does not appear on the sync client folders on any other device for you or other users.

Selecting a Sync Folder

Syncing files and folders automatically backs up your local data to Amazon WorkDocs. You can sync all files and folders or choose specific files or folders, which allows you to avoid syncing large amounts of data unnecessarily. Keep the following notes in mind when selecting a folder:

- You can only sync files that are included in your Amazon WorkDocs sync folder. Amazon WorkDocs sync does not support selecting folder outside of the Amazon WorkDocs sync folder.
- If the Amazon WorkDocs sync client is registered to a folder that includes files, they are updated as the latest versions of the files. To avoid overwriting online files with files synced from your desktop, select a new empty folder as your Amazon WorkDocs sync folder.

To remove files and folders from your computer, de-select them in **WorkDocs Selective Sync Settings**. This removes them from your computer, but they remain available for other users. You can still access them from the web client and your other computers.

To select sync folders during setup

1. Begin the Amazon WorkDocs setup process.

2. When you are prompted to choose files to sync, choose **Sync only the files and folders I select from WorkDocs** or **Sync all file and folders from WorkDocs**.

To sync specific files or folders after setup

1. Open the context (right-click) menu for the Amazon WorkDocs icon in your taskbar (or menu bar if you use macOS).

2. Choose the gear icon to open **Preferences** and choose **Select files and folders to sync**.

3. Select the check boxes for the items to sync. You can expand the top-level folders to select subfolders and individual documents.

4. To sync all new folders and files that you create in the future, choose **My Documents**, **New Folders And Files**, **Update**.

Uninstalling the Sync Application

You can uninstall the Amazon WorkDocs sync application from your local device without affecting the files that were last synchronized to or from your sync folder. These files and folders are no longer automatically updated after you uninstall the sync client, and you can delete them at any time.

To uninstall the Amazon WorkDocs sync application for Windows

1. In Control Panel, choose **Programs and Features**, **Amazon WorkDocs**, **Uninstall**.

2. When prompted for confirmation, choose **OK**.

3. (Optional) Delete the files from your sync folder.

To uninstall the Amazon WorkDocs sync application for macOS

1. Open the context menu for the Amazon WorkDocs icon in your menu bar.

2. Choose the gear icon to open **Preferences** and choose **Quit WorkDocs**.

3. Open the **Applications** folder.

4. Drag the Amazon WorkDocs icon to the trash.

5. Empty the trash.

6. (Optional) Delete the files from your sync folder.

Troubleshooting Sync Issues

The following are common issues and fixes with the Amazon WorkDocs sync client. For further assistance, you can contact Support or post on the AWS forum.

Topics

- Files Are Not Syncing
- Obtaining the Amazon WorkDocs Sync Client Log File

Files Are Not Syncing

If your files are not syncing, you can check for the following issues:

- Excluded files in the sync folder. For more information about file naming restrictions, see Excluded Files and Folders.
- File naming collisions. Ensure that each file name is unique.
- Selective sync preventing sync. Verify your selective sync settings and ensure that your folder is selected.
- Internet connectivity issues. Syncing resumes after internet connectivity is resumed.

Obtaining the Amazon WorkDocs Sync Client Log File

To further troubleshoot issues with the Amazon WorkDocs sync client, you may be asked to provide your Sync activity logs to help investigate and resolve your issue. You can do so with the following steps:

Obtaining the Amazon WorkDocs sync client log files

1. Open the context (right-click) menu for the Amazon WorkDocs icon in your taskbar (or menu bar if you use macOS).

2. Choose the gear icon to open **Preferences** and choose **Send Diagnostic Logs**.

3. In the description field, include the following information:

   - Short description of the problem
   - Full path of the affected documents or folders
   - Names of affected users

4. Choose **Submit**.

Amazon WorkDocs Drive

For Microsoft Windows users, Amazon WorkDocs Drive provides a native experience in Windows File Explorer for accessing all Amazon WorkDocs content. With Amazon WorkDocs Drive, users get the power of the AWS Cloud on their desktops. They can access all of their folders and files with minimal use of local storage. Users don't need to change the way they work, because they can see all of their folders and files in Windows File Explorer, which works just like the other files and folders on their desktop.

Amazon WorkDocs Drive is available for Windows PC users and for Amazon WorkSpaces. Amazon WorkDocs Drive can upload and download file sizes of up to 5 TB each, and allows file path lengths of up to 260 characters.

Topics

- Installing Amazon WorkDocs Drive
- Using Amazon WorkDocs Drive
- File Icons
- Enabling Offline Access
- Troubleshooting Amazon WorkDocs Drive

Installing Amazon WorkDocs Drive

If you have administrator privileges on your Windows device, you can install Amazon WorkDocs Drive.

Amazon WorkDocs Drive is available for Microsoft Windows 7, 8, and 10+, and Microsoft Windows Server 2008, 2012 R2, and 2016.

Amazon WorkDocs Drive requires Microsoft .NET library version 4.6.2 or newer, and HTTPS access on port 443 for all IP addresses for AWS.

To install Amazon WorkDocs Drive

1. Download Amazon WorkDocs Drive from https://amazonworkdocs.com/en/clients.

2. Follow the installation prompts, including entering the name of your Amazon WorkDocs site.

3. Your Amazon WorkDocs content appears as mounted drive W: on your computer.

Administrators who are responsible for managing the domain-joined machine fleet for their organization can install the Amazon WorkDocs Drive client by using Group Policy Objects (GPO) or System Center Configuration Manager (SCCM) Tools.

Note
When deploying with GPO or SCCM tools, we recommend installing the Amazon WorkDocs Drive client after users have logged in.

The MSI installer for Amazon WorkDocs Drive supports an optional install parameter that pre-populates the Amazon WorkDocs site information for users during registration; for example:

SITEID :*site-name*

Using Amazon WorkDocs Drive

You can access Amazon WorkDocs Drive from your Desktop shortcut. It also appears as mounted drive W: in Windows File Explorer.

You can perform operations directly from File Explorer, including creating, renaming, moving, and deleting files and folders. Moving files and folders out of Amazon WorkDocs Drive moves them into your Amazon WorkDocs **Recycle bin.**

To work with files and folders

1. Open File Explorer on your computer, and go to the W: drive.

2. Right-click an Amazon WorkDocs file or folder, choose **Amazon WorkDocs Drive**, and choose one of the following actions:

   - To generate a link to share the content with other users, choose **Copy web link**.
   - To view or edit the content in a web browser, choose **Open in browser**.
   - To allow specific users in an organization to access the content, choose **Share by invite**.
   - To mark a file or folder as a favorite, choose **Add to Favorites**.
   - To prevent other users from changing the file while you're working on it, choose **Lock**. When you're done, choose **Unlock**.

3. Your changes are automatically uploaded to Amazon WorkDocs and made available on all of your devices.

To search for content in Amazon WorkDocs Drive

1. Choose the Amazon WorkDocs Drive icon in the system tray and left-click to open the **Search** dialogue box.

2. Enter search terms to search for files in Amazon WorkDocs and open the files directly from Amazon WorkDocs Drive on-demand.

File Icons

Amazon WorkDocs Drive provides the following visual icons to communicate file status:

- **Blue arrow icon**—A file is syncing to the cloud.
- **Blue cloud icon**—A file is stored in the cloud.
- **Green checkmark icon**—A file is stored locally on your device.
- **Blue star icon**—A file or folder is marked as a Favorite.

Enabling Offline Access

You can enable offline access to your files and folders using Amazon WorkDocs Drive.

To enable offline access to files and folders

1. In File Explorer, select a file or folder and choose **Add to Favorites**.

2. Right-click on the Amazon WorkDocs Drive icon in your Windows system tray.

3. Choose **Keep Favorites on this Device**.

Files or folders marked as favorites are synchronized to your device from Amazon WorkDocs.

To turn off this option, choose **Remove Favorites from this Device**.

You can also temporarily pause the syncing of Amazon WorkDocs content to your device, and resume syncing later. If you have limited network bandwidth for syncing, you might consider using this option.

To pause file and folder syncing

1. On your computer, right-click on the Amazon WorkDocs Drive icon in your Windows system tray.

2. Choose **Pause**.

3. To resume syncing your files and folders, choose **Resume**.

While syncing is paused, you can continue working on downloaded files that are available on your local device. When syncing resumes, your changes are uploaded as new versions.

Troubleshooting Amazon WorkDocs Drive

Troubleshooting tips for the most commonly encountered Amazon WorkDocs Drive errors are listed below.

Recovered Files

If you don't have permissions to edit a file, you can't upload it to the Amazon WorkDocs site. Your changes are saved in your local `Recovered files` folder, and you can upload the file to Amazon WorkDocs as a new file.

Report an Issue

Choose **Report an issue** from the Amazon WorkDocs Drive settings menu to provide a description of the problem and send logs. This generates a tracking number, which you can include with the support case to help troubleshoot the issue.

Amazon WorkDocs Sharing Permissions

Amazon WorkDocs controls access to folders and files through the use of permissions. Permissions are applied based on the role of the user.

Topics

- Roles
- Shared Folder Permissions
- File Permissions
- Shared File Permissions

Roles

Both folder and file permissions are granted based on user roles. The following are the roles defined by Amazon WorkDocs that apply to folders:

- Folder owner – The owner of the folder or file.
- Folder co-owner – A user or group that the owner designates as the co-owner of the folder or file.
- Folder contributor – Someone who the folder has been shared with, without limited access to the folder.
- Folder viewer – Someone who a folder has been shared with, but has been given limited access (view only) to the folder.

The following roles apply to files:

- Owner – The owner of the file.
- Co-Owner – A user or group that the owner designates as the co-owner of the file.
- Contributor – Someone who has been asked for feedback on file.
- Viewer – Someone who a file has been shared with, but has been given limited access (view only) to the file.
- Anonymous viewer – A non-registered user outside of the organization who can view a file that has been shared via an external viewing link. Unless otherwise indicated, an anonymous viewer has the same permissions as a viewer.

Shared Folder Permissions

The following are the permissions defined by Amazon WorkDocs for shared folders:

- View – View the contents of a shared folder.
- View sub-folder – View a sub-folder.
- View shares – View the other users a folder is shared with.
- Add sub-folder – Add a sub-folder.
- Share – Share the top-level folder with other users.
- Revoke share – Revoke the sharing of the top-level folder.
- Delete sub-folder – Delete a sub-folder.
- Delete top-level folder – Delete the top-level shared folder.

Permissions for shared folders

Permission	Folder owner	Folder co-owner	Folder contributor	Folder viewer
View	X	X	X	X
View Sub-folders	X	X	X	X
View Shares	X	X	X	X
Add Sub-folder	X	X	X	
Share	X	X		
Revoke Sharing	X	X		

Permission	Folder owner	Folder co-owner	Folder contributor	Folder viewer
Delete Sub-folder	X	X		
Delete Top-level folder	X			

File Permissions

The following are the permissions defined by Amazon WorkDocs for files that are not in a shared folder:

- View – View a file.
- Delete – Delete a file.
- Annotate – Can add feedback to a file.
- View Shares – View the other users that a file is shared with.
- View Annotations – View feedback from other users.
- View Activity – View the activity history of a file.
- View Versions – View previous versions of a file.
- Download – Download a file. This is the default permission. The ability to download shared files can be allowed or denied in the file properties.
- Prevent Download – Prevent a file from being downloaded.
- Upload – Upload new versions of a file.
- Share – Share a file with other users.
- Revoke Sharing – Revoke the sharing of a file.

Permissions for a file not in a shared folder

Permission	Owner/Co-Owner	Contributor	Viewer	Anonymous Viewer
View	X	X	X	X
View Shares	X	X	X	X
Download	X	X	X	
Annotate	X	X		
View Annotations	X	X		
View Activity	X	X		
View Versions	X	X		
Upload	X	X		
Delete	X			
Prevent Download	X			
Share	X			
Revoke Sharing	X			

Shared File Permissions

The following are the permissions defined by Amazon WorkDocs for files in a shared folder:

- View – View a file in a shared folder.
- View Shares – View the other users that a file is shared with.
- Download – Download a file.
- Annotate – Can add feedback to a file.
- View Annotations – View feedback from other users.
- View Activity – View the activity history of a file.
- View Versions – View previous versions of a file.

- Upload – Upload new versions of a file.
- Delete – Delete a file in a shared folder.
- Prevent Download – Prevent a file from being downloaded. This is the default permission for files in the folder.
- Share – Share a file with other users.
- Revoke Sharing – Revoke the sharing of a file.
- Private Comments – Owner/co-owner can see all private comments for a document, even if they are not replies to their comment.

Permissions for a file in a shared folder

Permission	Folder Owner/Co-Owner	File Owner*	Folder Contributor	Folder Viewer	Anonymous Viewer
View	X	X	X	X	X
View Shares	X	X	X	X	X
Download	X	X	X	X	
Annotate	X	X	X		
View Annotations	X	X	X		
View Activity	X	X	X		
View Versions	X	X	X		
Upload	X	X	X		
Delete	X	X	X		
Rename	X	X	X		
Prevent Download	X	X			
Share	X	X			
Revoke Sharing	X	X			
See All Private Comments**	X	X			

* The file owner, in this case, is the person who uploaded the original version of a file to a shared folder. The permissions for this role apply only to the owned file, not all files in the shared folder.

** File owner/co-owner can see all private comments. Contributors can only see private comments that are replies to their comments.

Document History

The following table describes important additions to the *Amazon WorkDocs User Guide*.

- **Latest documentation update:** June 21, 2018

Change	Description	Date Changed
Hancom Online Editing is available. Create and collaboratively edit Microsoft Office files from the Amazon WorkDocs web application.	Hancom Online Editing	June 21, 2018
Open with Office Online is available. Collaboratively edit Microsoft Office files from the Amazon WorkDocs web application.	Open with Office Online	June 6, 2018
Amazon WorkDocs Drive is available for all Windows PC users. Enable offline access for Amazon WorkDocs Drive	Amazon WorkDocs Drive	April 2, 2018
Various changes to the web client interface	Amazon WorkDocs Web Client	February 22, 2018
Filter feedback, resolve feedback, and turn off email notifications	Giving Feedback	November 17, 2017
Amazon WorkDocs Drive is available for all Amazon WorkSpaces customers and in limited preview for Windows PC users	Amazon WorkDocs Drive	November 14, 2017
Instantly open and edit files with the Amazon WorkDocs Companion app	Adding and Editing Files	October 26, 2017
View activity for an entire site	Viewing the Activity Feed	September 13, 2017
Share a link	Share a Link	August 24, 2017
Lock and unlock files	Locking and Unlocking Files	May 24, 2017
Mobile enhancements	[See the AWS documentation website for more details]	April 25, 2017
Commenting enhancements	[See the AWS documentation website for more details]	March 10, 2017
Delete shared folders and files	Deleting Shared Folders and Files	January 18, 2017
Multiple features	[See the AWS documentation website for more details]	November 22, 2016
Selective file and folder sync	Selecting a Sync Folder	May 7, 2015
Multiple features	[See the AWS documentation website for more details]	April 28, 2015
Single sign-on support	Enabling Single Sign-On	March 31, 2015
Shared sync folder	Using the Shared Sync Folder	December 9, 2014
Phone apps	[See the AWS documentation website for more details]	November 20, 2014
Multiple features	[See the AWS documentation website for more details]	November 3, 2014

Change	Description	Date Changed
Initial release	Initial release.	July 10, 2014

www.ingramcontent.com/pod-product-compliance
Lightning Source LLC
LaVergne TN
LVHW082041050326
832904LV00005B/262